WELCOME HOME™

Kaffe Fassett

WELCOME HOME
Kaffe Fassett

copyright © 2010 Landauer Publishing
A division of Landauer Corporation
3100 101st Street, Urbandale, IA 50322
800-557-2144; www.landauercorp.com

President: Jeramy Lanigan Landauer
Vice President of Sales & Operations: Kitty Jacobson
Managing Editor: Jeri Simon
Graphic Designer: David Jordan
Contributing Editor: Candace Ord Manroe
Photography: Debbie Patterson; Craig Anderson Photography

This book is printed on acid-free paper.
Printed in China   10 9 8 7 6 5 4 3 2 1

Library of Congress Control Number: 2010926609
ISBN: 978-0-9825586-8-3

Contents

Making a House a Home

Softening the Scene

Setting the Stage

Creating the Mood

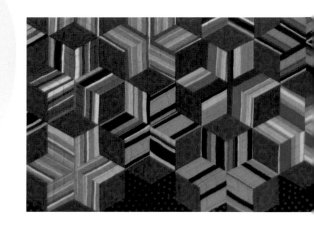

Museum Tour

Projects and Creativity

Foreword

KAFFE FASSETT

Kaffe Fassett enjoys worldwide artistic recognition for his visionary, organic and instinctive uses of color and pattern inspired by centuries of decorative arts and the compelling world of nature. Rather than peeling layers from an overcrowded world to create restful spaces, he integratesthe chaos. Ideas emerge that are transformed into paintings, textile prints, needlepoint, patchwork and knits. He is the first textile designer to be given a one-person show at both the Victoria and Albert Museum in London, and the Minneapolis Institute of Arts.

Welcome Home Kaffe Fassett stands out among his more than 14 books as the only one that takes readers into his home and studio to wander around and glimpse the incubator that is his world— drawers filled with old and new textiles, chests of china pots, shelves of marquetry and tin boxes, collections of fans and beaded bags, masses of colorful books on decorative arts.

He also is a leading fabric designer for Rowan Patchwork and Quilting and the leading knitwear designer for Rowan Yarns.

Born and raised in San Francisco, Kaffe moved to London to paint at the age of 19. He became a permanent London resident in 1964 and from London, travels, exhibits and teaches around the world.

"Color and pattern are my obsessions, and playing with them in different mediums leads to a stimulating life."

Introduction

Working with Kaffe Fassett and his studio is always a great joy for me. In 1995, Kaffe's lecture here at the Minneapolis Institute of Arts was quite well received. So, a year later when I was asked by Dr. Evan Maurer, the Museum's director, to develop an exhibition suitable for the opening of our new First Bank gallery, I immediately thought of Kaffe Fassett. His work would have broad appeal and excite an audience with little or no background information about textiles, as well as satisfy the more traditional museum visitor who frequently has considerable knowledge about the subject.

The instantaneous pleasure derived from seeing something created by this artist is an emotional lift experienced by almost everyone who comes in contact with his work. For those with training in the arts, particularly in the design and textile fields, more than just emotions become engaged. From November of 1997 to mid-February of 1998, when Kaffe Fassett's work was on view here at the Museum, I would frequently visit the exhibition and be intellectually stimulated and inspired by the subtle use of color and line, and the integrated artistic sensibility in each piece.

This book should prove a double joy for the reader. At first glance, enjoy the sheer pleasure of visual delight. Look again, but more carefully, to discover, understand, and appreciate the many levels of artistic expertise incorporated into Kaffe Fassett's work. Would that all learning could be made such a positive experience!

Lotus Stack
Curator Emerita, Textiles Department
Minneapolis Institute of Arts

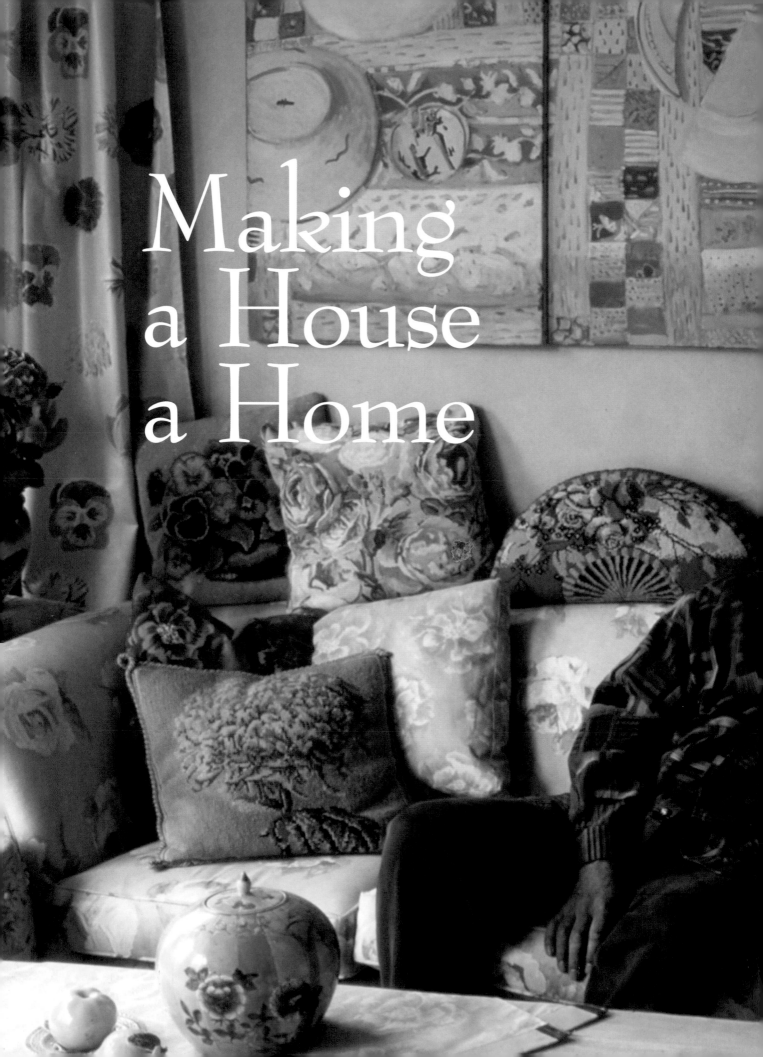

Making
a House
a Home

If the distinguishing difference
between a house and a home lies in
the details, the three-story
Edwardian residence of artist
Kaffe Fassett is unequivocably
a home. Details abound upon each
wall, window, shelf, and floor; in
every corner and cupboard; and
upon each furnishing and fabric
of his London domicile.
As one-of-a-kind imprints of the
homeowner, all of the details stand
as a single, unanimous testament:
This is clearly, proudly, Kaffe's
home. Not even a mirror could
prove more telling.

Changing Rooms

Born in San Francisco in 1937, Kaffe first moved to London to paint at age 19, relinquishing a scholarship to the Museum of Fine Art School in Boston after only a 3-month stint. He returned to London, this time to reside permanently, in 1964.

"I came to Britain because I liked the sense of humor and clarity of thought," Kaffe explains. "Soon I fell in love with the soft light, love of gardens, and lack of hype. This allowed me to develop my craft without someone commercializing it before it was fully formed."

That craft—Kaffe's modest appraisal of what is surely art—is fully formed today, even by his own exacting standards. It extends beyond painting, his constant love, to include the textile arts of needlepoint, quilting, and fabric design, for which he has become world-renowned.

But how does all that relate to making a house a home? Very simply. Kaffe uses each of these mediums to personalize his house. In fact, his entire home is something of a studio—or at least a test canvas—where his latest ideas and innovations are experimentally displayed in ever-changing combinations.

Left: An original Kaffe Fassett triptych distinguishes the living room wall in Kaffe's London home. The inset photo shows the same area in one of its altered stages.

Preceding Page: The yellow-background chintz curtains "Fassett's Flowers" and sofa fabric "Fresco Rose" are part of Kaffe's Rosamundi line for Designers Guild.

Above: Two very different looks of the same fireplace wall in the living room attest to the changeability of a room when color and pattern choices are made not just for furniture and accessories but walls as well.

Left: Kaffe gathered shards during walks across Hampstead Heath, a London park area, to fashion his first mosaic—his living room fireplace. He designed and painted the tiles inset into the mosaic, and also made the mosaic pot on the hearth.

11

Changing Rooms

Left: In Kaffe's paint studio, one of the walls features a collage he designed for one of his many books. At that time the room was used as a bedroom, below, but as his needs change so do the rooms.

"The house is like a constantly changing set," Kaffe says. "As I need a background for a new chair, a set of cushions, or a theme for a chapter in one of my books (he has written several on his textile arts), I will paint or paper the walls, or cover them with fabric, lay in new carpets, arrange needlepoint chairs or crockery or whatever, to achieve a look." Some rooms remain a bit more constant than others. "The leaf dining room, and rose-painted living room—these give the house a certain sense of continuity," he explains.

Kaffe constantly conceives new designs, which manifest themselves in products from mosaic kits to quilt designs, needlepoint projects to licensed fabric lines, on to all sorts of household items from ceramic teapots to placemats, and his rooms reflect the full sweep of his creativity. Color schemes change; motifs change; textures change; rooms change. But Kaffe's design style remains intact, despite the diversity: "You could call my style 'thoughtful kitsch' or 'embarrassment of riches' or 'the more the merrier.' Lavishly layered in pattern on pattern, in a palette that seems to span the spectrum, Kaffe's style is always rich.

Even one of the downstairs rooms is likely to undergo a disarming change of appearance, depending on the style, colors, and theme Kaffe's work is taking at the moment. What once was a bedroom, above, is now the mosaic studio, left. The vibrant patchwork wallpaper collage is effective, inspiring, and equally at home in either setting.

Function First

Just because Kaffe's rooms are so visually rich doesn't mean they exist for aesthetics only. They first and foremost must be hard-working. Nothing illustrates this better than the space known as the "Nerve Center"— the main office desk situated between the painting studio and the fiber studio, on the third floor.

Brandon Mably, Kaffe's studio manager and fellow designer, works here. Although the space clearly is all about work, it's also about fun—and, always, about good design.

"A room should function, but be amusing and lively to the eye at the same time."

Left: An eccentric collection of finds from Kaffe's worldwide travels includes treasured miniature vegetable teapots from Thailand, plus a humorous photograph of Kaffe and Brandon with Sister Scolastica from Germany, which appeared on their '98 Christmas card.

Opposite: Brandon Mably— studio manager and fellow designer—takes care of business at the "Nerve Center."

Function First

Kaffe not only insists that his rooms be functional, but he also demands that each furnishing pull its weight, accomplishing something besides merely occupying space. Kaffe is an avid reader, who constantly draws from his impressive collection of books for ideas and design inspiration. To accommodate the overflow of volumes, he made efficient use of a hallway wall by outfitting it with shelves.

Not surprisingly, many of Kaffe's furniture choices are case goods—cupboards, armoires, shelving units— with intrinsic storage capacity. Instead of dressing a hallway with a decorative console table, which has limited function, a tall cupboard is Kaffe's preference.

Above: French and English kitchenware atop a book shelf project the strong graphic design so prized by Kaffe.

Left: An unstudied air pervades Kaffe's hallway library. Books appear to be read and used, not just purchased and forgotten. Even the orderliness of a library isn't beyond a touch of humor in Kaffe's design. Kaffe's collection of slides, chronicling his many travels, add shape, form, and color contrast to the vertical volumes.

Not only does the cupboard, left, offer closed-drawer storage, it also has open shelving for an artistic presentation of Kaffe's favorite collections. Kaffe's collections span a vast range, reflecting his diverse interests. "Mostly strength and romance in design attracts me," he says. Those qualities are especially apparent in blue-and-white pottery (a mix of English and Oriental), which is featured in compelling still-life vignettes throughout the house.

Above: Kaffe found this pair of Victorian portrait vases in an antiques shop near Washington, D.C.
Left: A massive pine cupboard with several fabulous collections of pottery adds intense drama to the first-floor hallway.

Function First

Kaffe's attention to color, composition, and collectibles thrives as well in his work studios as it does in his living spaces.

Kaffe's first needlepoint design was commissioned by Pamela Lady Harlech for Lord Harlech. Since then, his commissions have included department stores, cruise liners, Elizabethan houses, American theaters, and even a tapestry weaving company in Scotland. Since 1978, he has been the leading needlepoint designer for Ehrman Tapestries of London. Here, working on a flower series, Kaffe finds all his materials close at hand. In his at-home fiber studio, supplies are conveniently stored in a succession of tall, colorful, faux-finished chests along one wall and in a bevy of baskets overflowing with richly colored yarns along the opposite wall.

Left: Soft afternoon light filters into the third-floor studio window where Kaffe needlepoints a flowered pillow design.

Those walls in the fiber studio that aren't covered by the tall, whimsically finished storage chests are still hard-working, both visually and functionally. Kaffe's paintings are dotted across one wall, teaming up with a work-in-progress quilt and its different colorways. The combination of permanent and transitory seems exactly what's needed for an eye-pleasing arrangement.

Left: The Tumbling Blocks quilt fragments led to a complete quilt. Inspiration for the new quilt? An old one.

19

Creative Containment

One of the secrets to Kaffe's successful storage of objects out in the open is to keep the grouping free-flowing, or at least to suggest as much. His is rather the opposite of a rigid, tightly controlled look: books aren't sectioned off according to height, but are allowed to stand together in a looser fashion, directing the eye up and down in joyful, swinging rhythm. The end result is not only greater visual interest, but an appearance of greater authenticity, too. Kaffe's groupings maintain an innocence which stands in direct opposition to a "decorated" look.

More than any other room in the home, the kitchen typically poses the biggest storage challenge (unless the owner happens to be a textiles artist—then storage is an issue throughout). Kaffe solves the problem visually, as one might expect. Instead of exclusive behind-closed-doors storage, he opts for front-and-center displays as well. Decorative plates march along the wall at near-ceiling height; bowls, teapots, and planters mingle on a top shelf; and a bright assembly of mismatched cups fills the shelf below—some cups standing neatly side-by-side, others hanging from old-fashioned cup hooks. An assortment of exotic teas and condiments that are either prettily packaged or same-shaped to form an eye-pleasing combination sits on the lowest shelf.

Right: Kaffe's home is not without sets of matching china, but his painter's eye finds beauty in the mismatched. "A room should function, but be amusing and lively to the eye at the same time," he says.

Creative Containment

What in less skilled hands might amount to clutter manages to be a decorative tableau. In Kaffe's living room, the vibrant hues of seemingly hundreds of different patterned textiles peek out from cupboard drawers and cubby holes and spill over chairs and onto the floor. But instead of appearing unruly, the medley looks so good that it's clear it must be intentional.

Kaffe reinforces that intentional look by assembling a collection of ceramics in the same space, repeating the full-gamut color palette. A flea-market chair, cleaned, painted, and featuring his own one-of-a-kind needlepoint design, picks up the air of exuberance, pulled in close to the hodgepodge of textiles.

Right: Bursting at the seams with colorfully patterned textiles, a living room storage cabinet becomes a focal point when topped with a crown of ornate pottery and china.

Ever mindful of storage needs, Kaffe even put the awkward area beneath the staircase to utilitarian function, outfitting it with a storage cabinet, which he then integrated into a mural design. Of course, besides functionality, the area provides a surface for displaying art.

"Mostly strength

and romance

in design

attracts me."

Left: *Kaffe chose to cleverly cover the once dark staircase niche in fool-the-eye fashion with original floral paintings on canvas by London needlepoint artist Jill Gordon.*

Creative Containment

But back to the question, how does Kaffe make his house a home? Most importantly, he uses it to its fullest. Every nook, cranny, and surface area has a purpose and a function. An area such as the mosaic room tends to get dusty, dirty, and messy at the snap of the tile cutting tool, so supplies are stored in pots, bulging boxes, and colorful stacks. In other rooms, storage comes in countless ways. In the fiber studio, Kaffe stacked found dressers on top of each other to create a wall of storage drawers, taking the opportunity to enhance the surfaces with a faux-marble treatment done by a friend from Holland. Baskets and bowls from all over the world overflow with balls and hanks of Rowan yarn in every texture, thickness, and color. Even a chair seat is called upon to hold a pile of folded fabrics—a display seemingly casual and spontaneous, but one that clearly articulates Kaffe's keen eye for color, pattern, and texture.

"I am basically a painter

and have shows every few

years," says Kaffe.

"I squeeze it in with

everything else, between

promo travels, designing

textiles and mosaics, and

writing books."

Opposite: Supplies for mosaic work are stored in easy-to-find piles and boxes.

Right: Current fabrics in a stack on a chair make a colorful fashion statement when the fabrics are as engaging as Kaffe's designs for Westminster Fibers.

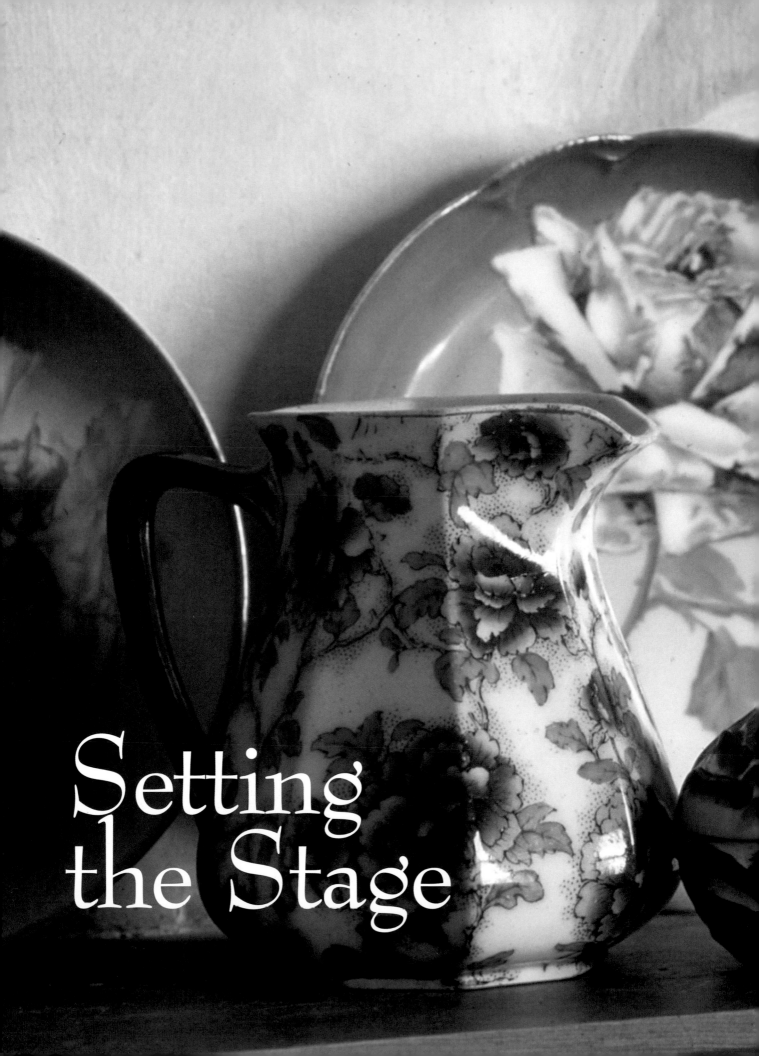

Setting the Stage

To Kaffe, every surface of his home is an invitation to decorate. Each wall, counter, cupboard—even the fireplace—is a blank canvas awaiting whatever pattern and palette he might favor at the moment. The specific decorative looks will change, but one thing remains constant: Nothing goes unadorned—or even colored only in solids (much too tame an approach for Kaffe's taste). Pattern is a must, whether it's an intermittently applied floral design scattered across a wall, or the ragged-edge geometry of odd-shaped mosaic tiles.

Different Strokes
Strokes

As the main public area of his home, Kaffe's living room is an arena for showcasing his latest creative efforts. But it's also a place for harnessing his creative energies. His current wall decoration is a case in point. The handpainted roses on the living room's pale, antique-yellow walls inspired "The Rosamundi Rose" furnishing fabric collection Kaffe designed for Tricia Guild's Designers Guild.

The wall treatment shows Kaffe's sensitivity to site—the mellow patina of the buttery paint suggests a vintage appropriate for an Edwardian building. (Plus, yellow is the quintessential English color—and an easy, cheery one to live with, day to day.) Over the yellow, Kaffe handpainted big, splashy old-fashioned roses, setting a theme to be repeated on rugs and furnishings.

Right: Kaffe even continued his handpainted floral pattern onto the window, as a bright garland cascading down from the window top.

"Perhaps I am heading toward a slightly simpler arrangement with softer colors. I don't really have a future mapped out. Old worlds and the texture of aging inspire me."

Left: Proof of Kaffe's bold mastery of color is in his juxtaposition of the vibrant crimson chair against the pale yellow walls. The rose pattern repeats on both the needlepoint-covered chair and on the wall—a violation of Decorating 101 that Kaffe pulls off with success.

Different Strokes

One of Kaffe's most ingenious wall treatments decorates the angled cubby beneath a staircase. Instead of dismissing this as "dead space," as many home owners would, Kaffe saw an opportunity for artistry. And, this time, not even his own. Cleverly, he adapted the floral still-life paintings on canvas of talented English needlepoint artist Jill Gordon to serve as a form of wall paneling. He sized and cut picture mouldings to fit around the paintings, with the end result being a sort of trompe l'oeil mural: the bouquets appear to be murals painted directly onto the wall. But Kaffe isn't content with only displaying the work of a fellow artist. In his kitchen, he wields the brushes and paints the cabinets himself, decorating the doors with the blue-and-white pottery patterns he admires so much as a collector.

Right: When mounted to the walls with picture moulding, Jill Gordon's masterful artwork looks convincingly mural-like.

Above and right: Kaffe often tells his students to "just play with the colors." Putting his inspiring words into practice, he painted the kitchen cabinets while the production crew for this book was on location: On Day 1, we took a photograph of the plain cabinet doors, right. On Day 3 Kaffe started putting color into the outlines he had drawn, far right. On Day 5 the cabinet doors were done, above.

Finishing with Fabrics

Creative paint applications are only one way to dress a wall. Kaffe is equally comfortable cloaking his walls in fabrics—especially fabrics he has designed. And because all of Kaffe's designs begin as paintings, his finished fabrics bear a distinct painterly quality that distinguishes them from other prints. Kaffe's fondness for floral motifs, for stylized but recognizable renderings of his subjects, and for audacious mixes of color, are all evident in his fabrics.

Always apparent is Kaffe's
signature way with color—
never uniform or singular,
but a masterly blend of
shades, tones, and
seemingly incompatible
hues, for a palette of
deep complexity.

Left: Kaffe celebrates color,
pattern, and floral motifs
throughout his home, from his
floral rag rug (his own design) to
his needlepointed chair (again, a
Kaffe design).
Opposite: Colors on this
room's wall fabric are repeated on
the chair and in accessories for
lively results.

Papers Plus… Collage

Color is the key to Kaffe's successful blending of diverse materials and motifs. No matter how many colors he combines within a single design or within a single space, Kaffe makes the mix work. One way is by keeping all the colors close in value, so that none pops out as stronger than the others. When that occurs, Kaffe can then contradict his own formula for success, adding a small decorative accessory that features colors of a different value—for example, the brightly dressed doll in a soft, pastel setting on the staircase landing.

Left: A still-life painting illustrates Kaffe's design principle concerning color: Keep all values close, for can't-miss visual harmony. The wallpaper, designed by Kaffe, helps set the stage.

Above: The striped wallpaper in the paint studio is the perfect counterpart to an elaborately patterned chair.

Opposite: Flavia, a doll made by Kaffe, is a colorful standout in this pastel setting, which features Kaffe's wallpaper as a backdrop. The repetition of what Kaffe terms "high blue" is his explanation for the success of the color mix.

Papers Plus…Collage

If Kaffe subscribes to any design rule, it's "no rules, please"—or at least that's the message communicated by the astonishing decorative surfaces in his home. Who ever said a single wall must be covered in a single material, be it paint, wallpaper, or fabric? Certainly not Kaffe. Proof is his "scrap" wall—a layer upon layer collection of wallpapers, fabrics, and original color sketches. And if that's not enough, he even tops the montage with a china-painted plate—a sure sign of this artist's confidence in his skills at mixing mediums. Kaffe's home features other scrap collages. Most notable is a four-panel folding screen in the dining room that he made using magazine cut-outs, wallpapers, and other materials that caught his eye.

Above: A sense of artistic imagination thrives on this scrap wall designed by Kaffe. Pinned onto wallpaper remnants is the original color sketch he made for his "The Rosamundi Rose" furnishing fabric for Designers Guild.

Left: Flowered postcards all pieced together create yet another version of wallpaper.

Opposite: A robust autumn palette prevails in the dining room, which features decorative items designed by Kaffe, including a folding collage screen and a brilliant garden-themed quilt.

Tile Cool Surfacing with Tile

Pattern takes many forms, and Kaffe is fascinated with exploring the possibilities presented by tiles. Mosaics composed of irregularly shaped shards achieve the most variety, but even surfaces covered in uniformly sized square tiles offer opportunity for forming pattern through organization of different colors and glazes.

Laying tiles from light to dark, or intermixing cool and warm tones, creates visual rhythm. In his bathroom, Kaffe covered countertops and vanities with multicolored tiles, creating interesting plays of light and dark, bright and dull. He enhanced visual interest by varying the sizes of the tiles from one surface to another.

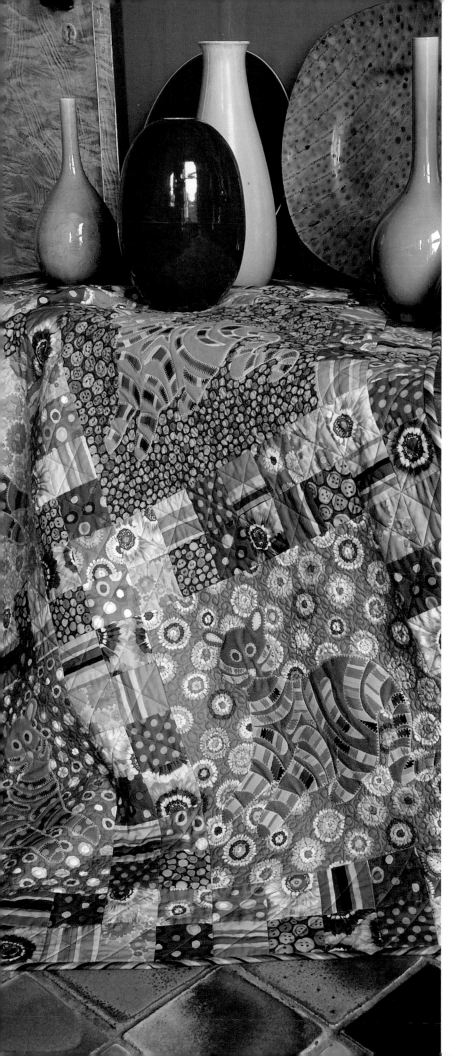

Opposite: Antique hand-beaded bags, one of Kaffe's favorite collectibles, beautifully complement the palette of blues and greens on a tiled surface.

Left and Below: Two sizes of tile in the bathroom provide double the impact. The lively rhythm created by placing tiles according to color is an ancient approach to pattern.

Cool Surfacing with Tile

How to place layer upon layer of pattern, color, and material within a single space without creating chaos? Kaffe's secret lies in careful, discreet integration of contrasting decorative elements into a unified whole. Each material, in some subtle way, relates to another in the space. Even a wall treatment as seemingly minor as a mosaic backsplash border in the kitchen was thoughtfully conceived. The watery blues, pale jade greens, and creamy white tiles echo the colors in the room's wallpaper— another Kaffe creation. And, the mosaic ties into collectibles on display in the room, especially Kaffe's favorite—blue and white English and Chinese pottery. One of the beauties in being something of a Renaissance artist like Kaffe is being able to inter-relate themes between various design mediums. Kaffe's kitchen wallpaper design featuring blue-and-white china relates to his mosaic tiles and, at an even more basic level, to the collectibles that inspired it.

Right: A ceramic tile backsplash topped with a small-tile mosaic border lends unity to the assortment of blue-and-white pottery pieces in the kitchen.

Even negative space is an invitation to decorate to an eye as insightful as Kaffe's. Using broken bits and pieces of pottery he had gathered during strolls through Hampstead Heath, he replaced the gaping hole of his living room fireplace with a mosaic fire screen. To add order to the mishmash of pieces, Kaffe inset ceramic tiles he painted with pottery motifs in blue and white. The tiles provide a visual connection to the blue-and-white vases, urns, and other ceramics displayed on the mantel shelf.

Left: Handpainted tiles on the fire screen repeat the forms of pottery displayed on the hearth and mantel. Kaffe gave an ordinary vase a facelift with a hand-applied mosaic treatment, then centered it on the hearth to lend continuity to the tile-and-mosaic fire screen just behind it.

Making the Most of Mosaic

Some rooms lend themselves to the cool hand of tiles better than others. In the bathroom, tiles are especially welcome for their rugged durability and tolerance of water. But in Kaffe's bathroom, an ordinary application is out of the question. His bath, dressed top to bottom in white-and-cream mosaic tiles, gains extraordinary handcrafted style with little oddities such as tiny mirrors and teapot lids. Kaffe not only designed the mosaic himself, but he applied it as well, covering all four walls and the ceiling. Even when working with a monochromatic (single color) palette, Kaffe ensures depth by varying the shades and tones of his chosen color (in this case, neutral white-cream).

Opposite, Above, and Left: An Old World—even Moorish—ambience is formed in the bath by covering all surfaces in mosaics using irregularly shaped cream and white china shards. Kaffe included a special backsplash border behind the sink as part of the mosaic, and framed a mirror using darker-hued bits of tile.

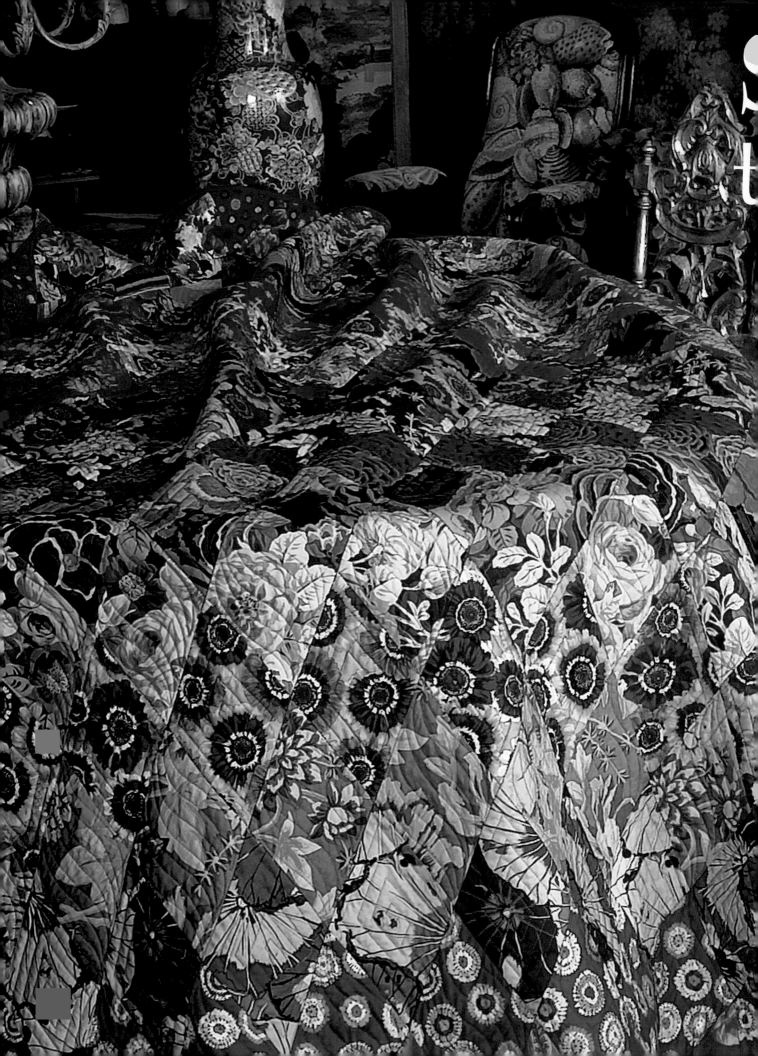

oftening e Scene

How to get away with so many pattern combinations, so much color intensity, such a labyrinth of visual intrigue? One way is by softening the setting. And Kaffe is expert at it. He masterfully fills his rooms with sink-down upholstered furnishings and stacks of cushy pillows. Hard surfaces such as tabletops are softened with thick, quilted comfort. Hard walls are softened with fabric coverings and more—fabric- and paper-covered screens are positioned just so, transforming the walls into softer, three-dimensional surfaces.

Pattern and Color

Dining at Kaffe's place takes a natural course, with organic-motif fabrics featured center stage. Kaffe's popular floral designs appear as the main fabrics in the vibrant diamond-patterned quilt covering the dining table. The use of diamond shapes on more than one furnishing helps to unify the multi-patterned room. Note the mix of textures as well as scale and shape relating the diamond-patterned mosaic to a tumbling blocks needlepoint pillow. Gerbera daisies add a burst of singular focal color. What is more appropriate than stunning sensory stimulation in a space intended to whet the appetite for both food and conversation?

Left: Kaffe uses an abundant harvest of fruit, vegetable, and flower motifs in decorating. Their patterns bind them together into an organic mix of fabric, needlepoint, majolica, and painted panels.

Opposite: A diamond floral motif unifies the dining room. The coordinating fabrics are part of Kaffe's popular patchwork-fabric range.

Below: Current fabrics in a stack on a chair make a colorful fashion statement when the fabrics are as engaging as Kaffe's designs for Westminster Fibers.

Pattern and Color

Kaffe doesn't ignore hard surfaces such as ceramic collectibles, wood cabinets, or plaster walls as areas for introducing color and pattern, but it's the soft furnishings that make all his efforts at color and pattern approachable. A large pink rose motif splashed across a vivid crimson background might intimidate with its strong color and design—but not as a needlepointed upholstery fabric for a chair. Instead, what could be intimidating becomes inviting. The needlepoint's pink roses are a transitional thread connecting a mix of patterns—from the pastel roses on the walls and sofa to the exuberant floral pattern underfoot on the rug.

"I do love to mix different textiles, scales, and mediums if the color and patterns relate. I am always looking for harmony in imperfect juxtapositions. Mixtures bring life to the color schemes."

Above: Fabric-on-fabric makes a soft bed for colorful ceramics, while also providing transition between them and the floral fabric on the living room sofa.

Opposite: The textural appeal of the flamboyant rag rug Kaffe hooked softens the boldness of its design.

Pattern and Color

Brightly colored flowers are a recurring theme Kaffe calls on throughout his home. Part of Kaffe's success in personalizing spaces lies in his unusual presentations. To introduce color and pattern, he groups flower-motif beaded bags in a big bowl. (Because of their exquisite hand-craftsmanship, as well as their looks, beaded bags form one of Kaffe's premier and prized collections.)

Another display unlike any other is Kaffe's still-life assortment of rose-themed fabrics, wrapping papers, tinware, porcelains, woven bags, books, and cards. Laid out with the front panels of a vest-in-the-making, the odds-and-ends pieces form a visually cohesive and pleasing arrangement.

Not one to be satisfied with a gorgeous but temporary arrangement, Kaffe continuously puts color pencils to paper to sketch a display that will last forever.

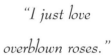

*"I just love
overblown roses."*

Opposite: *Beaded bags
feature the same deep
shadowing on flowers that
Kaffe creates on his
needlepoint designs.*
    Left: *Two of the rose
fragments in this pretty
vignette are the front
parts of a petit-point
waistcoat Kaffe designed
for his 1999 flower-theme
show in New York City.*

51

Pattern and Color

Inspirations from nature as hard and solid as stone go soft around the edges with Kaffe's artistry, in the form of needlepoint pillows. He displays the inspiration and the art together, intensifying the character of each through contrast. Colors in the pillow's yarn palette are eminently stonelike—muted, the color of rain, yet subtly varied for a range of shades and tones within a monochromatic palette. Even here, where the look goes quiet and gray, nothing is quite as simple as it appears—nuances of color imbue depth and richness.

Right: The hard geometry of a living room corner is softened by a tabletop display including two needlepoint pillows of Kaffe's design. The painting just behind the table also is by Kaffe. This vignette illustrates Kaffe's adeptness at working within a monochromatic (single color), neutral palette.

Below: Kaffe's quilt and mosaic both have the muted coloration of age. He says: "I just put stuff together 'till they sing—if not, I try some other combination."

Taking inspiration from a Dutch painting featured in Kaffe's book, *Glorious Inspirations,* Kaffe's studio workers hand-needlepointed both a chair and stool in a strikingly beautiful seashell motif. Shown in front of a Kaffe painting that also features a natural colorway with hints of yellow and lavender, the needlepoint pattern mixes seamlessly. Yet another textile— a quilt mounted over the wall— brings a smaller-scale geometric print to the mix. Tiles on a tabletop echo that geometry, and also the faded browns and blues.

"I do love to mix different textiles, scales, and mediums if the color and patterns relate," says Kaffe. "I am always looking for harmony in imperfect juxtapositions. Mixtures bring life to the color schemes."

Left: A rusty-red background on the antique area rug accentuates the reddish hints found in the painting and on the chair fabric.

Quilts, Pillows, and Rugs

In quieter spaces, Kaffe leaves behind the glittering jewel tones and diverse pattern mixes for a more soothing sensibility. Earthy colors— browns, creams, rusts with hints of sand and sky fill these spaces. In a private corner, a rag rug decorates a calm sitting area. In a living area, several softening touches combine— from the Schoolhouse quilt draping a comfortable couch that serves as a perch for perfectly blended needlepoint duck pillows— to the well-worn geometry of a faded floor rug.

"Mixtures bring life

to color schemes."

Left: The rag rug "Mischievous" is by Brandon Mably.

Opposite: Chinese ancestors mix an ancient world with a Schoolhouse quilt featuring Kaffe's current fabric collections.

Quilts, Pillows, and Rugs

A quick and easy way to soften spaces is with decorative throw pillows. Given Kaffe's fondness for changing the look of his rooms, the portability of pillows becomes especially attractive. Pillows can be tossed upon a chair to add instant color and pattern. But when that look bores, they can be tossed elsewhere (even in the closet) and replaced with others that strike an entirely different note. Because of their relatively small size, pillows also are ideal canvasses for displaying hand-craftsmanship. Kaffe's needlepoint patterns are particularly popular—in his own home, as well as among the public.

Above: Pillows in a stack—storage on a chair. A tower of pillows makes a fun fashion statement when the fabrics are as attractive as these—Kaffe's designs for Designers Guild.

Left: Richard Womersley, Kaffe's business partner, wove the throw that's covering the chair, providing a perfect perch for Kaffe's needlepoint Rooster pillow.

Opposite: One of Kaffe's favorite flowers, the gazania, decorates his fabric design, which covers pillows and is repeated in the quilt.

Quilts, Pillows, and Rugs

Like the Jericho walls of the song, those in
Kaffe's home tumble down when covered
with Kaffe's Blue Star quilt. The pattern
cascades down the wall with intense
energy—energy heightened by a palette
Kaffe calls "full blooded." Rich and warm,
it extends to every other element within
the quilt's proximity: the chair, pillows,
even the flowers seem
to radiate energy. By
keeping all the
furnishings' fabrics
the same intensity, the
vibrant mix succeeds.

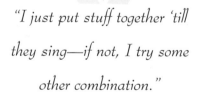

"I just put stuff together 'till

they sing—if not, I try some

other combination."

Right: *The antique chair gets a
new covering in one of Kaffe's
needlepoint patterns.*
Opposite: *This still life consists
entirely of designs by Kaffe, even
including the rag rug. The Blue Star
Quilt is bordered in Kaffe's Spots
fabric. The pillow features a
needlepoint center and a
mosaic border.*

Creating the Mood

Any room can feature this wall color and that furniture fabric; this style of window treatment and that kind of sofa. So what's to distinguish one room from another—or, more to the point, someone's room from anyone else's? The answer lies in the personal details: a home needs to reflect the interests of its occupants. Professional interior designers know this well and take time to learn their client's preferences on the smallest level, for it's the only thing that saves even the best designs from looking canned. In Kaffe's home, one-of-a-kind personal details that attest to his passions abound—memorabilia from favorite places, collections reflecting his love for various forms or patterns. Every square inch within every room reveals some facet of Kaffe's taste, character, and talents, to make his living spaces sing.

Inspiring Collections

If collections are one of design's most important aspects, it's essential to know how to create them. Not all vases grouped en masse create a collection. Kaffe's definition of a collection, despite its apparent looseness, hinges on some concrete criteria. First, objects must relate in type— paintings displayed with paintings, china with china. But that's not all. His grouping must relate thematically—these are paintings of china, or of stones, for example. And to qualify as a collection

of paintings in one of Kaffe's rooms, the group also must relate in color—the palette of each painting must be compatible with those of the others.

But compatibility isn't entirely the answer: In terms of shape, variety is the better option. His canvases are a mixed bag of scale and shape, allowing the eye to dance around and better appreciate all the pieces within the grouping because of their diversity, not despite it.

Left: Here, Kaffe has hung a collection of paintings in, of all places, his textiles studio, because the room is long and therefore has more vista. Says Kaffe, "I can see at a glance how a show is shaping up, as I work on my textile projects."

Opposite: Kaffe's painting of a majolica still life, shown in the background, inspired this grouping of teapots and facilitiates the seamless transition from the wall to the objects on the table.

Teapots, as with his other collections, are acquired intuitively, not according to any prescribed plan. "Some find me as gifts, others I collect instinctively," he explains. Arranged together in layers, tiered by size, the teapots make teatime a conversation item, any time of day.

Inspiring Collections

Many of the collections giving unique character to
Kaffe's rooms have the Orient as either their origin
or their inspiration. This is mainly coincidental: it's
not the idea of the objects being oriental that
counts with Kaffe, as much as that they have an
appealing design or look. Blue and white
colorations especially appeal to him and they star
in still lifes throughout his house. Kaffe doesn't
limit himself to two-tone ceramics, though, as
displayed in the rounded forms of smiling
Buddhas, with the Zen men issuing joy from a
living room window.

*Above: Most of Kaffe's smiling
Buddhas are more than 100 years old.*
*Left: Unity in color but diversity in
shape—a combination of English
and oriental china makes a strong
graphic statement.*

Color is the foundation for many of Kaffe's groupings of artful accessories. Blue is a favorite foundation—yet, as seen from these two examples, it can present strikingly different results. Blues, appreciated as solids with no other colors competing, go rich and oceany on art-glass pottery. The clean shapes of these bottles and vases are shown to their best advantage against a blue mosaic wall and tabletop.

An entirely different mood is achieved by another grouping of blues that has a big temple jar as its focal point. The temple jar connects the disparate items in the group—a painting by Kaffe, as well as two temple jar needlepoint cushions and a swatch of temple-jar decorator fabric. "I know if I can paint something, I can justify the expense of buying it," says Kaffe. "This temple jar has figured in many tapestries, paintings, and fabric designs."

Left: The pattern on a blue temple jar is a favorite inspiration for many of Kaffe's designs.

Below: Echoes of the 1940s and 1950s can be seen in this blue themed vase collection.

Inspiring Collections

Adjusting a room's purpose presents no problem for Kaffe. What was once a bedroom now serves as his art studio. At certain times of day the light is perfect for carrying out painterly interpetations of one of his many collections, be it a selection of teapots, or a study in a pastel grouping of vases, bowls, and books.

It's interesting to note that at times a collection may inspire a painting, yet occasionally it's a painting that inspires another collection. Kaffe's vast store of vases, pots, and teapots allows him to mix and match to his heart's content in infinite combinations based on shape, color, or purpose.

Left: A small grouping of jars, vases, and books stars on a painting in progress. Their soft pastel colors proved to be the reason for their selection from the loaded cabinet.

"I know if I can paint something, I can justify the expense of buying it."

Left: *A cabinet full of decorative pots reflects Kaffe's fondness for certain shapes and patterns. Variety in size, shape, and type results in maximum visual interest. The pots rest in full view in Kaffe's painting studio, waiting to star on his canvasses. He uses them over and over in his still lifes.*

Accents and Accessories

Accents

Even stones—or especially stones—are signature design pieces to Kaffe's discerning eye. And therefore they merit a place in his home as prized collectibles every bit as legitimate as any others. The subtle nuances of pattern and color in objects from nature render them as decorative as the more brightly colored and boldly patterned florals Kaffe designed as needlepoint patterns. The effect is the same: the stones bring individuality to their area of display; the needlepointed florals make each chair they cover a stand-out. What's more, the differences between the two types of objects only increase the home's vitality, pleasing the eye with a range of textures, palettes, and patterns.

Left: Murky mauves and grays on river stones appeal to Kaffe's appreciation for variegated color.

Above and Right: Faux-Roccoco chairs from a London flea market receive one-of-a-kind attention from Kaffe. Each is painted a different color and covered in a different (but related) needlepoint design. Kaffe's designs were stitched by David Forest.

Accents and Accessories

One of the most telling testaments to a person's taste isn't the decorative objects they put on obvious display, but the utilitarian items such as their everyday dinnerware. Even here, Kaffe holds true to form, revealing himself as an inveterate mixer with little regard for anything matched. "We have some sets of china in the house," he confesses, "but I do love a motley collection of compatible plates." And coffee mugs. And bowls. And saucers. And teapots. And so on. Instead of hiding the hodgepodge behind closed doors, Kaffe seizes the opportunity to decorate his kitchen. Everyday wares are stored on open shelving, becoming collections in their own right.

In addition to introducing inimitable character through major focal points, Kaffe zooms in on the details, too. No corner of anything—be it wall, mantel, or tabletop—is too small to serve as an opportunity to project personality. An example of decorating down to the details is a collection of inlaid-wood and flower-theme boxes at one corner of a table—pure Kaffe.

Opposite: Kaffe designed this deliberately mismatched set of dinnerware with well-known English potter Rupert Spira. The seashell oilcloth is also Kaffe's design.

Below: Kaffe's collection of boxes includes tin, marquetry, and Chinese parchment.

"Being a poor artist when I arrived in London, I bought cheap, broken, and damaged but very pretty, objects and placed them all together in pleasing arrangements—making still lifes actually."

Accents and Accessories

Not one to leave things halfway done, Kaffe tackles his small garden with as much gusto and ferver as he does his home. His chosen artform for this area, mosaic, allows him to create the patchwork-like look he enjoys working in the most. The inventive pieces stand up to the damp English climate and provide a splash of color during dreary days.

Large film cannister lids, a square of plywood, and a sewer pipe all have one thing in common—they're excellent surfaces for mosaic work.

Opposite: A clay sewer pipe and the lid of a large film cannister provide exciting shapes for Kaffe's foray into mosaics.

Left: Leaning up against a tree, purple and yellow pansies artfully fill a plain wooden board. A sealer ensures protection against dampness.

Above: Tile walks, mosaic pots, and lots of flowers provide Kaffe with a restful outdoor area.

73

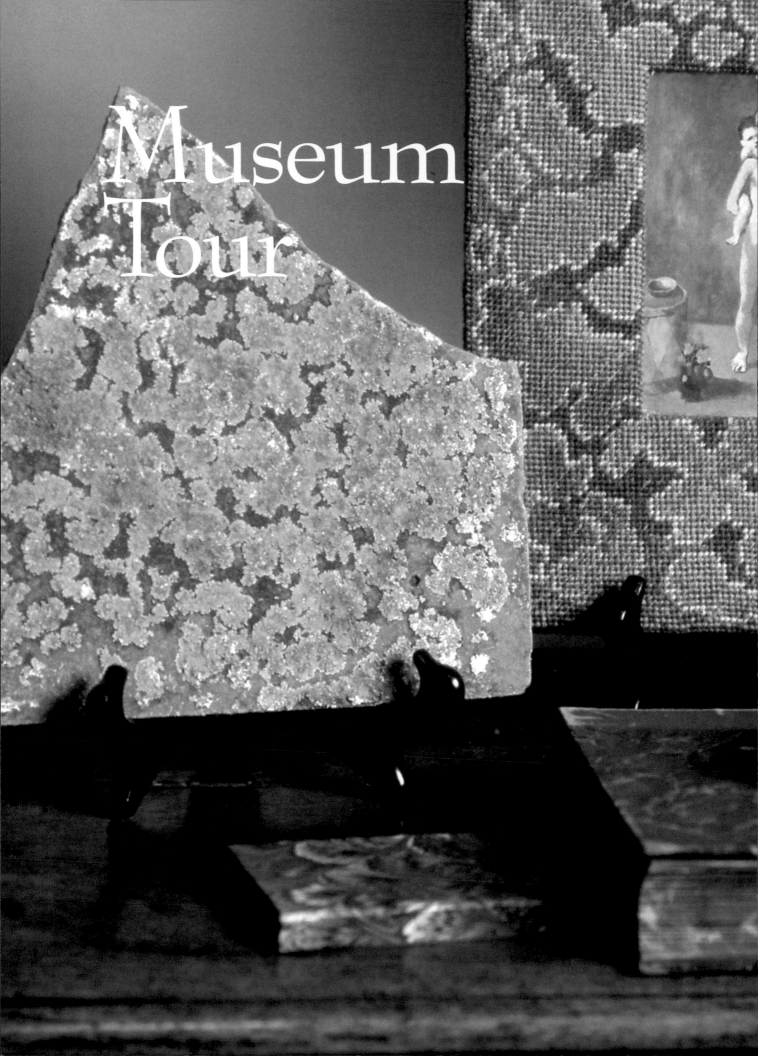

Museum
Tour

This museum
retrospective of Kaffe's
work looks familiar for
good reason—many of the
textile arts and accessories
featured are plucked
straight from his home.

Worldwide Influences

In 1988, the Victoria and Albert Museum in London hosted a retrospective exhibition of Kaffe's work, making him the first living textile artist to have a one-man show there. Since then, the show has traveled to Finland, Holland, Norway, Denmark, Sweden, Australia, and Canada. Finally, in 1998, it made its way to the USA. The images shown in this chapter are from the Minneapolis Institute of Fine Art, which presented the show in great detail. The layers of pattern and texture against the coral red background, below, reflect Kaffe's fascination with oriental richness. Opposite, needlepoint flowers and bold knits mix seamlessly with the museum's Chinese chair.

Life Imitates Art or Art Imitates Life?

In this case, the dividing line is blurred. The vignettes on these pages capture the essence of the exhibition, which is all about integrating Kaffe's textiles into realistic home settings. Much of the show's charm lies in the approachable, as opposed to museum-like, atmosphere of the capsuled displays. At the center of the exhibition is a true-to-life rendering of Kaffe's at-home London studio, complete with artful inspirations tacked to a pinboard (top right, below, and below right). Kaffe's fruit and vegetable needlepoint pillows snuggle up warmly on the museum's antique European sofa (opposite).

Geometric Harmony

Simple, yes, but there's nothing plain about these geometrically intriguing pieces. The designs are bold, with richly resonant color and crisp pattern repeats. The museum's displays follow that cue, with each textile sample stretched, folded, or mounted to accentuate its linear definition. Be it patchwork, knitting, or needlepoint, Kaffe's fondness for geometric structure is clearly evident.

The tweedy palette of the vignette shown opposite reflects Kaffe's response to the gray light of England. The sampler blanket contains some of his first attempts at taking the yarns and "playing with color!"

A Striking Blend of Old and New

The museum staff's insight into Kaffe's work shows in every way. They custom-painted backgrounds for the various vignettes in eighteen different compatible colors (almost like home) and pulled just the right antique decorative pieces from the museum's archives to complement Kaffe's work. After all, so much of what Kaffe does is directly inspired by the history of decorative arts.

The tropical flower needlepoint, above, blends beautifully with the Museum's Japanese jar while a periwinkle blue background sets off the red and blue knits, opposite.

Projects
and Creativity

Interpretations of collections, images, and patterns all come together in Kaffe's inspirational sketch books. Using watercolors and brushes, felt-tip pens or color pencils, he fills page after page with trials of a certain motif or color scheme until it's just right. Only then does the pattern get translated into a needlepoint canvas, large mock-up for a patchwork or decorator fabric, or quilt or rag rug design. Many of the quilts, rag rugs, and pillows shown in the photographs are featured in this chapter for you to make and enjoy.

Quilts and Instructions

Diamonds Quilt

Materials

- 45-inch-wide 100% cotton fabrics by Kaffe Fassett:
  ¾ yard red Rings for the half diamonds border
  ½ yard each of: red Variegated Ivy, brown PomPom Dahlias, black PomPom Dahlias, bold Serape Stripe, red Rambling Rose, red Rustic Floral, rose painted Daisy, red PomPom Dahlias, red Shawl, rust Painted Daisy, charcoal Rustic Floral, dark Rosette, plum Bekah, violet Rambling Rose, purple Painted Daisy, green Rustic Floral, antique Lotus Leaf, rust Plink, and red Forest of Arden
  ¾ yard red Aboriginal Dots for binding
  6 yards backing
- Batting at least 3 inches larger all around than the finished quilt top
- Cotton quilting thread
- Templates OO, PP, QQ, and RR on pages 114–115

Size of Quilt

The finished Diamonds Quilt measures 78¾ x 90 inches. Quilting will reduce the final measurements.

Cutting

Note there are alternating long and short rows of diamonds. Not counting the border, there are ten long rows of fifteen diamonds. There are nine short rows of fourteen diamonds.

To cut the diamonds, cut a 5-inch strip from selvage to selvage. Use template OO to guide cutting the angles. It is a 60-degree angle.

Each row has only ONE fabric. For the Serape Stripe border, it is best to cut two 5-inch strips into diamonds and then with the leftover fabric cut a few diamonds a "bit" wonky so when you piece that row, the stripes will go in many directions.

For the border cut two template RR, 2 reverse template RR, 28 template PP, and 18 template QQ.

Piecing

Follow the diagram on page 88 for piecing.

For the first few joins, draw a seam allowance on the back of the diamonds and partial diamonds. They overlap in a peculiar way to make a quarter-inch seam so use the drawn line and pins to get it right. The quilt is sewn together in diagonal rows. Start in the upper left hand corner and sew each row. When all are sewn, then sew the rows together.

The diamond is a favorite pattern of Kaffe's and he uses it often in his knitting and quilting designs. Quilters will enjoy the challenge of finding just the right fabrics needed.

Quilts and Instructions

Finishing the Quilt

Press the pieced quilt top. Layer the quilt top, batting, and backing, and baste the layers.

Quilt in the ditch. Fill the border with loops. For the long rows, work inward following the shape of the diamond with ½-inch between lines. Fill the short rows with shallow wavy or S lines.

Trim the quilt edges and attach the binding.

Diamonds Layout Diagram

Welcome Home Stars Quilt

Materials

- 45-inch-wide 100% cotton fabrics by Kaffe Fassett:
    3 yards periwinkle Aboriginal Dots
    2½ yards purple Spot
    1 yard each of: antique, bold, green and red Serape Stripe
    6 yards periwinkle Aboriginal Dots for the backing and binding
- Batting at least 3 inches larger all around than the finished quilt top
- Cotton quilting thread
- Templates A, B, C, and D on pages 116–117

Size of Quilt

The finished Welcome Home Stars Quilt measures 65 x 92 inches. Quilting will slightly reduce the final measurements.

This is a VERY DIFFICULT quilt to make. There are many set in seams. It is important to follow the diagram in piecing the vertical rows together as it makes it possible to avoid trying to do set in seams on the sharp points of the stars.

Cutting Borders

From the periwinkle dot fabric used around the edge, cut the borders first. Cut 2 lengths 3 x 87½-inches for the side borders. Cut 2 lengths 3 x 65½-inches for the top and bottom borders.

Stars and Diamond Shapes of the Background

Cut 3½-inch wide strips from selvage to selvage. Using template A as a guide, cut the diamonds. Cut 144 background diamonds.

Each star takes six diamonds. Most strips will give eight to ten diamonds. Make most diamonds from six identical stripes. Make a few from the leftovers. These unpredictable diamonds make the quilt more interesting.

Cut enough to make 60 stars.

Wow! What a fun way to play with striped fabrics! One of the "labor of love" quilts we sometimes hear about, this one's absolutely worth the effort. The graphic effect is dazzling and the deep gorgeous colors take on a starring role.

Quilts and Instructions

Triangles (Half Diamonds)

From the background fabric, cut 3½-inch-wide strips.

   Cut 118 template B.
   Cut 8 template C and 8 template C reversed.
   From the periwinkle dot fabric,
   Cut 28 template B.
   Cut 2 template C and 2 template C reversed.
   Cut 6 template D and 6 template D reversed.

Piecing

   It will be necessary to arrange the stars on a design wall to keep them in the long vertical rows. There are only half stars in each vertical row. Once those vertical rows have been assembled, they are sewn to the next vertical row and only then do you get whole stars.

Look at the diagram and make the units exactly as shown. Follow the diagram and sew the units together step by step, in the order indicated. The goal is to do set in seams on the blunt angles and never on the sharp angles of the stars.

Adding the Border

   Once the quilt top is assembled, sew the two side borders to the center. Then, sew the top and bottom borders to the quilt top.

Finishing the Quilt

Press the pieced quilt top. Layer the quilt top, batting, and backing, and baste the layers. Quilt in the ditch of each star, then ½-inch and 1-inch inside. Stitch ½-inch inside each background diamond. Fill border and adjacent matching triangles with loops.

   Trim the quilt edges and bind with the background fabric.

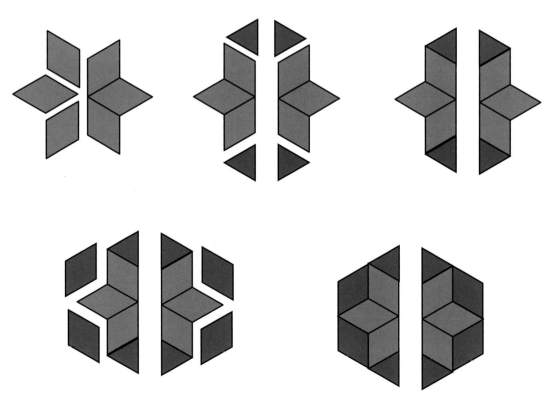

Star Assembly Diagram

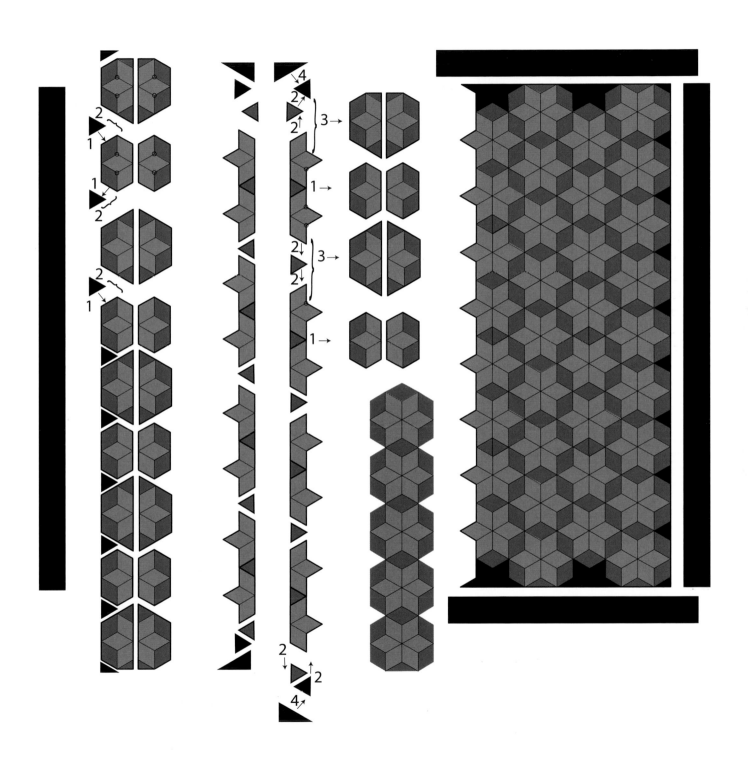

Welcome Home Stars Layout Diagram

Quilts and Instructions
Quilts

Katzahyden

Materials

• 45-inch–wide 100% cotton fabrics by Kaffe Fassett:
   ½ yard each of: olive Rings, blue Cogs, ochre Buttons, green Plink
   ⅛ yard each of: Shot Cotton in clementine, peasoup, lipstick, and curry, bold Serape Stripe, red Serape Stripe, red Rings, and magenta Spot
   ¼ yard each of: purple green Painted Daisy, and green Serape Stripe
   ½ yard ochre Diagonal Stripe for the binding
   3¼ yards for the backing
• Batting at least 3 inches larger all around than the finished quilt top
• Bright colored cotton quilting thread
• 2 yards Steam a Seam Lite (16-inches wide) or similar light weight fusible web
• 1 sheet translucent template plastic, at least 10 x 14-inches
• Cat pattern on pages 118-119

Size of Quilt

The finished Katzahyden Quilt measures 45 x 45 inches. Quilting will reduce the final measurements.

Making the Blocks

Note that some cats face one direction and some the other. Because of this be sure to use the picture as guidance and cut the cats and the stripes as shown. Use the front and reverse side of the template plastic to make the cats facing each way.

Draw the cat shapes onto template plastic using a dark permanent marker and the patterns on pages 118-119. Using a pencil, trace each cat outline onto the paper backing of the fusible web. Remember to trace 2 facing one way and 2 facing the opposite. Trace the stripes onto the leftover web pieces. Cut out the cat shapes about a quarter inch outside the drawn line. Put numbers on the stripes that correspond to the drawing and cut them out about a quarter inch beyond the drawn line. Following the manufacturer's directions, fuse the cat shape to the wrong side of the fabric. Fuse the "stripes" to the coordinating fabric in the same way. Be sure to pay attention to the direction of striped fabric to get the best effect. It looks best if the striped fabric runs crosswise on the cat stripes.

Cut out the shapes on the pencil outline.

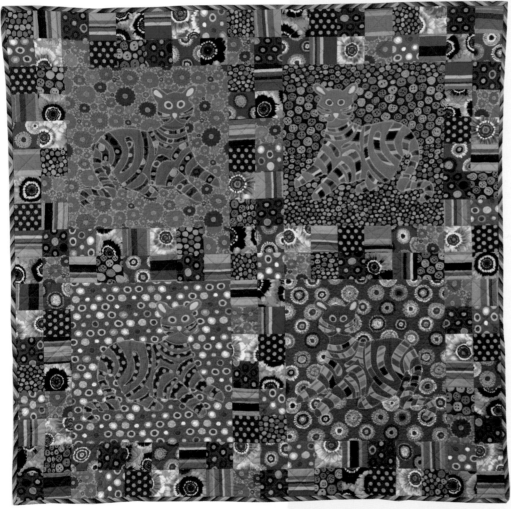

Appliquéd cats playfully 'hide' while surrounded by vibrant colors in this fun block quilt. Simple shapes make this quilt easy to create.

Designed by Rebekah Lynch

Quilts and Instructions

Cut a coordinating background fabric 16 x 16-inches (the finished size is going to be 15-inches, but cutting it a bit too big helps when the appliqué stitching shrinks it a bit). Find the center of the background fabric. Remove the paper backing from a cat and place the center of the fused backed cat onto the background. Iron to adhere. Cut out the cat's stripes and using the template plastic as a guide, place each stripe on its place and iron to adhere. Select two eyes for each from the rings fabric. Find colorful bits to use for ears and nose and treat all in the same manner as the stripes.

Using a bright colored contrasting thread, do a buttonhole or zigzag stitch around each cat, each stripe, each face feature AND stitch into the cat to make the leg haunch and the jowls.

Trim the block to 15½ x 15½-inches.

Making the Sashing

Using all the fabrics except the solid shot cottons, cut 180 squares 3 inches each. Sew six long horizontal sashes, using 18 squares in each. Sew 6 short vertical sashes using 12 squares in each. Keep the colors random and nicely spread out.

Assembling the Top

Sew two short vertical sashes together making a long strip, two squares x 6 squares. Make six of these.

Sew one vertical side sash piece to the left side of block 1, and do the same to blocks 2, 3, and 4. Sew block 1 to 2. Sew block 3 to 4.

Sew two long horizontal sashings together making a long strip 2 squares x 18 squares. Make 3 of these.

Sew a horizontal sash to the top of blocks 1-2, to the bottom of blocks 1-2 and to the bottom of blocks 3-4. Sew the units together.

Press.

Finishing

Make a sandwich with the backing, batting, and top. Using a green thread, freehand quilt small loops over the background of the blocks. Quilt diagonal lines through the squares in the sashing. Do not quilt through the cats. If desired, freehand quilt a name for each cat in the background near it.

Trim the quilt edges and bind with the bias cut stripe.

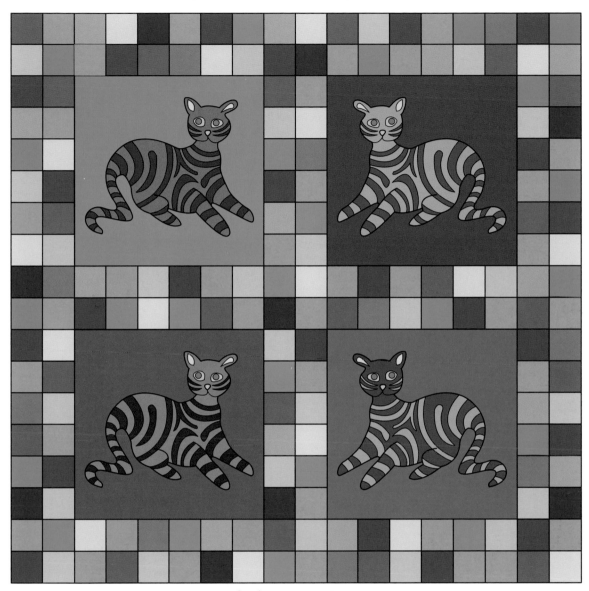

Katzahyden Layout Diagram

COMBINATIONS

Cat 1 (upper left)
Background: Cogs—blue
Cat: Shot Cotton—curry
Stripes: Rings—red

Cat 2 (upper right)
Background: Buttons—ochre
Cat: Shot Cotton—peasoup
Stripes: Serape—red

Cat 3 (lowr left)
Background: Rings—olive
Cat: Shot Cotton—clementine
Stripes: Spot—magnta

Cat 4 (lower right)
Background: Pink—green
Cat: Shot Cotton—lipstick
Stripes: Serape—bold

Schoolhouse Quilt

Materials

- 45-inch-wide 100% cotton fabrics
  by Kaffe Fassett:
  2½ yards gold Roman Glass for cutting
      borders lengthwise
  2 yards byzantine Roman Glass;
      use leftover for binding
  1¼ yards eucalyptus Shot Cotton
  1 yard rust Plink
  ¾ yard each of: brown Millefiore,
      olive Rings, and brown Guinea Flower
  ½ yard each of: China blue Spot, dusty
      Cogs, brown Cogs, and black Suzani
  ¼ yard pumpkin Paperweight
  5⅓ yards backing
- Batting at least 3 inches larger all around
  than the finished quilt top
- Cotton quilting thread
- Templates J, K, and L on pages 120–121. In
  addition to these, make the following:
  Template M: 2 x 7½ inches
  Template N: 2 x 2½ inches
  Template O: 2 x 3½ inches
  Template P: 2 x 5½ inches
  Template Q: 2½ x 4¼ inches
  Template R: 2½ x 3½ inches
  Template S: 2½ x 2¾ inches

Size of Quilt

The finished Schoolhouse Quilt measures 63½ x 90½ inches. Quilting will slightly reduce the final measurements.

Shapes

The Schoolhouse blocks all use the same shapes. The actual-size templates J, K, and L are on pages 120–121.

Cutting

There are 24 House blocks. Each has a main color, an accent color, and a background color.

In all the blocks the background is the same fabric, eucalyptus Shot Cotton. The houses are the following combinations:

Main fabric/Accent fabric
Brown Millefiore/dusty Cogs—4 blocks
Olive Rings/brown Cogs—3 blocks
Rust Plink/brown Guinea Flower—2 blocks
Black Suzani/brown Millefiore—4 blocks
Slate Spot/rust Plink—4 blocks
Brown Guinea Flower/olive Rings—4 blocks
Dusty Cogs/pumpkin Paperweight—2 blocks
Brown Millefiore/brown Cogs—1 block

Kaffe has managed to rework an old (and sometimes tired) pattern into a breath of fresh air.

By using a rich amber and rust pallet, he's created a warm glow against teal blue on this village of houses.

Projects and Creativity

Quilts and Instructions

For each house cut the following:
Background fabric: 1 J, 1 Jr, 2 O, 1 P, 1 Q, 1 R, and 1 S
Main fabric: 1 L, 3 M, and 6 N
Accent fabric: 1K, 2 M, and 1 N

Lattice and Corner Pieces
From the byzantine Roman Glass, cut fifty-eight 2 x 12½-inch strips.
From the rust Plink, fussy cut thirty-five 2-inch squares so one dot is in each square.

Border
From the gold Roman Glass, cut two 4½ x 64-inch strips for the top and bottom edges and two 4½" x 83" for the side edges.

Making the Blocks
The Schoolhouse blocks are all made in the same manner but in eight different colorways.

Referring to the Schoolhouse block diagram, sew the N pieces to each end of the O pieces. Sew the resulting strips to three M strips, alternating the strips. For the front of the house, sew an N piece to one end of a P piece, making sure the N piece will face wrong side up in the pieced strip. Sew the resulting strip between two M strips, making sure the M strips will face wrong sides up.

Sew the front of the roof K piece to the side roof L piece, making sure the K piece will face wrong side up. Sew a J and Jr piece to each end of the roof. Sew this unit to the side and front wall unit, carefully matching the seams.

Sew the chimney N pieces to each end of the Q piece; sew the R piece to the left end and the S piece to the right end of the chimney unit. Sew this unit to the roof unit.

Make a total of 24 Schoolhouse blocks.

Adding the Lattice Strips
Following the layout diagram, opposite, scw a vertical lattice strip to the left side of each block. Take five corner pieces and four horizontal lattice pieces and sew together into a strip. Make a total of seven such strips.

Schoolhouse Block Diagram

Sewing the Blocks into Rows
Following the layout diagram, opposite, arrange the center portion of the quilt, making sure the blocks are placed in the correct sequence and placing the lattice strips between the rows.

When you've checked and double-checked the correct placement, pick up the first two neighboring blocks of each horizontal row, and sew together. Pick up the next block and sew to the unit. Repeat across, then sew a vertical lattice strip to the end of the row. Repeat for the remaining rows.

Assembling the Rows
Following the layout diagram, sew the block rows and the lattice rows together, carefully matching the seams.

Adding the Borders
Sew the long border strips to the side edges of the quilt top. Sew the strips to the top and bottom edges of the quilt top.

Finishing the Quilt
Press the pieced quilt top. Layer the quilt top, batting, and backing; baste the layers.

Quilt in the ditch in all the seams then ¼-inch inside the house front, house side, and roof front. Zigzag quilt down the center of the lattice strips. Quilt lines ⅝-inch apart on roof side following angle of roof. Quilt a swirl circle design in the border.

Trim the quilt edges and attach the binding.

Schoolhouse Layout Diagram

Great accessories are easy to come by—just make an extra block while you're making your quilt. From your fabric leftovers, cut circles for a yo-yo pillow, or strips for a bright border.

Materials

- Scraps of many different quilt fabrics
- ½ yard of fabric for the back
- Polyester pillow form
- Cotton quilting thread

Size of Pillow

The size of your pillow will depend on the size of the additional quilt block and any borders you may wish to add. Piping and ruffles add additional inches.

Fabrics and Color

The fabrics used for the pillow blocks are the same as you use for your quilt blocks. Choose a matching fabric for the backing. Leftover fabrics are great for covering piping cord, piecing a scrap border, or making yo-yos.

Shapes

The shape of the quilt blocks largely determines the shape of the pillow. Keep in mind that a purchased pillow or pillow form is easiest to work with—borders can be added until the right shape is achieved.

Cutting the Fabrics

Depending on the pillow you choose to make, either cut the pieces needed for one quilt block from the Schoolhouse Quilt, or cut forty-nine 5-inch circles from a variety of scraps. Keep some matching fabrics on hand for borders, piping, and/or ruffles.

Making the Pillow Top

Refer to the quilt instructions to make your pillow block. For yo-yos, turn under the hem of each fabric circle and sew a running stitch all around the outer edge. Making sure the right side of the fabric is the outside of the yo-yo, gently pull the thread, gathering the fabric until a small opening is left. Knot the thread. Working from the center out, attach the yo-yos to each other and onto a large square of fabric.

Finishing the Pillow

Add borders until the pillow top is the desired size. Cover piping cord with a strip of fabric or cut a ruffle twice the length of the circumference of the pillow. Sew the piping or ruffle around the right side of the pillow top.

For the pillow back, cut a piece of fabric in the same height but 5 inches wider than the widest part of the pillow. Cut the fabric in half and hem the cut edges with 1-inch hems. With right sides together and outer edges matching, sew the back pieces to the pillow top, overlapping the hemmed edges neatly in the center. Turn the pillow right side out and insert the pillow form.

Leaves Rug

Deep autumn-colored leaves form a

border around a bright blue pond

splashed with floating lily pads.

Rag Rugs

Because of the large individual loops and the simple hooking action, rag rugs are very quick to work. Begin with a simple one such as the Blocks rug, or dive into a somewhat more challenging one. Any one you choose will be a joy to work up due to the basic techniques described below. Rug hooking couldn't be simpler!

The materials that go into a rag rug are a good selection of scrap fabrics for your rag strips and a large piece of burlap for the rug foundation.

General Instructions

The instructions for each rug are identical, except for the measurements. Read through all instructions thoroughly before starting your rug.

Materials

For any one rug:
- Piece of loose-weave burlap—add a 5-inch margin to each edge of the size specified underneath each rug pattern.
- Variety of scrap fabrics for strips (see Choosing the Colors on page 107)
- Large rug hook
- 5 yards of 2½-inch-wide twill carpet binding (optional)
- Strong thread for hemming

Foundation Fabric

Burlap is the best foundation fabric for rag rugs. It provides a strong base and the threads are wide apart enough to accommodate the rug hook. Kaffe normally uses a heavy-weight, loose weave burlap with about 10 or 11 threads to the inch. When you purchase your burlap be sure to add 5-inch margins (10 inches total) to your width and length measurements.

Rug Hooks

The main tool you need for hooking a rag rug is a rug hook. Basically, there are two types of hooks—one with a latch and one without. Kaffe prefers working with the latch hook because it is easy to use. The latch is pushed upward when the hook is inserted down through the fabric and then pulled down as the hook is pulled up through the fabric, enclosing the rag strip. The opening and closing action of the latch prevents the hook from catching on the burlap.

Leaves Rug finished size: 27 x 45 inches

Roses Rug

A favorite design subject, the rose takes

center stage on this fun-to-make rug.

A scallop border contains the growth.

Rug Frames

Kaffe does not use a frame when hooking a rug. This makes the project portable and allows him to move around within the design, filling in various areas without having to reframe each time. He says: "My finished rugs may not be as absolutely rectangular as a rug worked in a frame, but this slight asymmetry is part of the charm of the hand-hooked rag rug."

If you prefer to use a frame, a large artist's stretcher frame will do the trick. Use thumb tacks to secure the section of burlap you are working on to the stretcher.

Choosing the Colors

Study the photograph of the rug to decide which colors to choose. You will need scrap fabrics in a wide variety of colors and in a range of tones. Look for scraps to match the photographed color scheme or match the colors to your home decor.

Picking the Fabrics

Most fabric scraps are suitable for rag rug strips. Rag rugs are great recycling projects. Save old clothes for a rug with built-in memories or pick up inexpensive garments at rummage sales and thrift shops.

Patterned fabrics are just as enjoyable to work with as plain, and they often produce a lovely mottled effect. Don't restrict your choice of fabric to a specific thickness or texture either. Varying textures and fabric weights adds interest to the allover design and keeps it from being too uniform. Kaffe tends to collect fabrics that go well with a specific color palette. But try to find a wide variety of colors in a range of dark, medium, and light tones. With a good selection on hand, you will be able to pick and choose suitable colors as your design progresses.

To make sure all your scrap fabrics are preshrunk before use, wash and dry them before cutting strips. If you have not been able to locate fabrics in some of the colors you need, you may want to dye some of the scraps beforehand.

Roses Rug finished size: 39 x 63 inches.
Instructions begin on page 104.

Blocks Rug

A study in color doesn't need to be
boring. Pull many fabrics that belong to
the same color family and have at it.

Preparing the Rag Strips

The width of the rag strip depends on the texture
you want in your rug, the thickness of the scrap
fabric, the size of your rug hook, and the weight of
the burlap. The best thing to do is to cut a short strip
of fabric and hook a few test loops. In general, Kaffe
cuts his rag strips between ½ inch and 1 inch wide,
the thicker the fabric the narrower the strip
should be.

In general, cut the strips on the straight grain
of the fabric, not on the bias; however, for a long
continuous strip, start cutting along an outside edge
and cut in a decreasing spiral toward the center of
the fabric.

Transferring the Design

Trace or copy the rag rug diagram of your choice. Using a pencil and ruler, divide the traced diagram in half horizontally and vertically, making equal quarters. Divide each quarter into smaller quarters.

Using dressmaker's chalk or a large needle with a long length of yarn, mark off the design area on the burlap, drawing only the outer outline to ensure a margin of burlap around your design area. Then divide the burlap design area the same way you did the diagram.

There are three methods to get the design onto the burlap: You can freehand-draw the design onto the burlap; draw the enlarged design directly onto the burlap square by square; or draw the design onto tracing paper, then transfer it to the burlap by using a hot-iron transfer pencil.

To copy the diagram square by square, use a felt-tip marker to copy an enlarged version of the diagram's design lines onto the burlap, following the diagram. Complete all the lines in one section before moving on to the next. Do not worry about making mistakes or corrections—the lines will be covered by the dense loops.

If you choose to enlarge the design on tracing paper, use a pencil to draw the outline and grid. To transfer the design from the tracing paper, first turn the paper over and, with a transfer pencil, retrace the center outline of the rug and the design lines (not the grid). Place the tracing paper on the burlap with the transfer-pencil side down. Using a hot iron, press the design onto the burlap following the instructions that come with the transfer pencil.

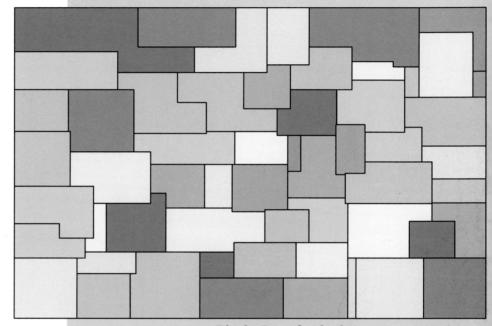

Blocks Rug finished size: 27 x 45 inches.
Instructions begin on page 104.

Mischievous Rug

Brandon Mably, Kaffe's business manager,

is a designer in his own right, as attested

by Mischievous the striped cat.

Hooking the Rug

Learning to hook a rug will take no time at all, especially when you use a latch hook. If you have never made a rag rug before, practice hooking on a scrap piece of burlap to determine the best widths for your strips and to decide on the height of the loops. Don't worry about making mistakes—you can pull the loops out if you make a mistake. After a completed rug has been walked on, it will be much harder to pull the loops out because the flattening of the rug pushes the loops together.

Some rug hookers prefer to work the loops underneath the burlap and some prefer the loops on top. Kaffe prefers to hook his loops on the topside of the burlap so he can see the design and color scheme materialize as he works.

If you are right handed, hold the hook in your right hand above the burlap and hold the rag strip in your left hand under the burlap. Lefties must reverse this action. Push the hook straight down through the burlap, making sure the entire latch goes through the fabric as well. Catch the fabric strip with the hook, enclose it with the latch, and pull the end of the strip through the fabric. Then insert the hook one or two fabric threads away from where it was first inserted. Pull the strip through again, this time forming a ¼- to ⅜-inch loop on the right side of the burlap. Continue making loops in this way, placing the loops close together but not overly tight. Kaffe's rugs generally have about seven loops to 2 inches.

When you come to the end of a strip or when you want to change colors, merely pull the end up to the right side of the fabric. Start the next strip about two fabric threads away from where the last strip ended. Do not insert the hook through the same hole as a previous loop or strip end or you might pull out a loop by accident. Trim the ends of the strips so they're the same height as the loops.

Which direction to work in is a matter of choice. Kaffe usually follows the shape of the design. For instance, on the Blocks Rug the loops are worked in straight lines, but on the Rose Rug the curved shapes are filled in with loops at random or in curves that follow the design line.

Finishing the Rug

A special advantage of rag rug making is that very little finishing is required. After completing the hooking, simply turn under the unworked burlap margins and hem, mitering the corners in the process. If desired, you can bind the rug with wide twill binding: trim the unworked edges to 2 inches and sew the twill binding next to the loops. Turn the binding to the wrong side and handsew in place with strong thread.

Mischievous Rug finished size: 34 x 41 inches.
Instructions begin on page 104.

Mosaics and Instructions
Mosaics

Materials

- Mosaic base of your choice, such as a plain vase, terra-cotta pot, or piece of plywood
- A variety of ceramic tiles, glass tiles, plates, cups, etc. Damaged goods are easy to find.
- Tile nippers
- Hammer
- Quick-setting floor- and wall-tile adhesive and grout or a premixed adhesive/grout product
- Protective eye covering

Breaking the Pieces

Using nippers, cut pieces from china plates, cups, etc. With the nippers you can actually cut small motifs from the china that you can then form into a pattern. To break tile, place between two towels on a board; tap gently with hammer.

Adhering to Base

An easy method for creating mosaics is to use a premixed product that combines adhesive and grout. Use it to secure pieces to the base, and to fill gaps between pieces. For delicate work, secure the shards with adhesive first, allow to dry, then apply grout. For a richer look, color grout with ink before using. Work grout between the pieces with a palette knife, then apply more grout with a damp cloth, wiping over entire surface for a smooth look. After the grout has partially set, wipe off excess with a clean, damp cloth. When grout is dry, polish shards with a paper towel. Apply a sealer, if necessary, to protect project from dampness.

China shards and broken tiles are turned into colorful accent pieces under Kaffe's talented hands.

Diamonds Quilt

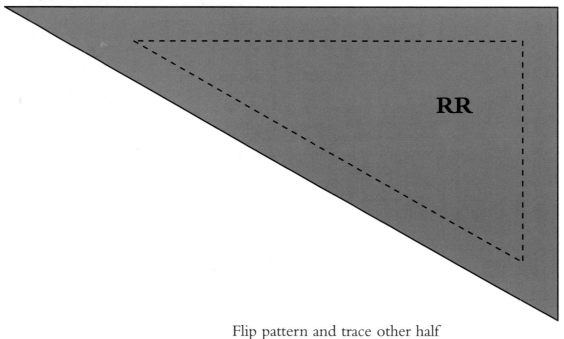

Flip pattern and trace other half

RR

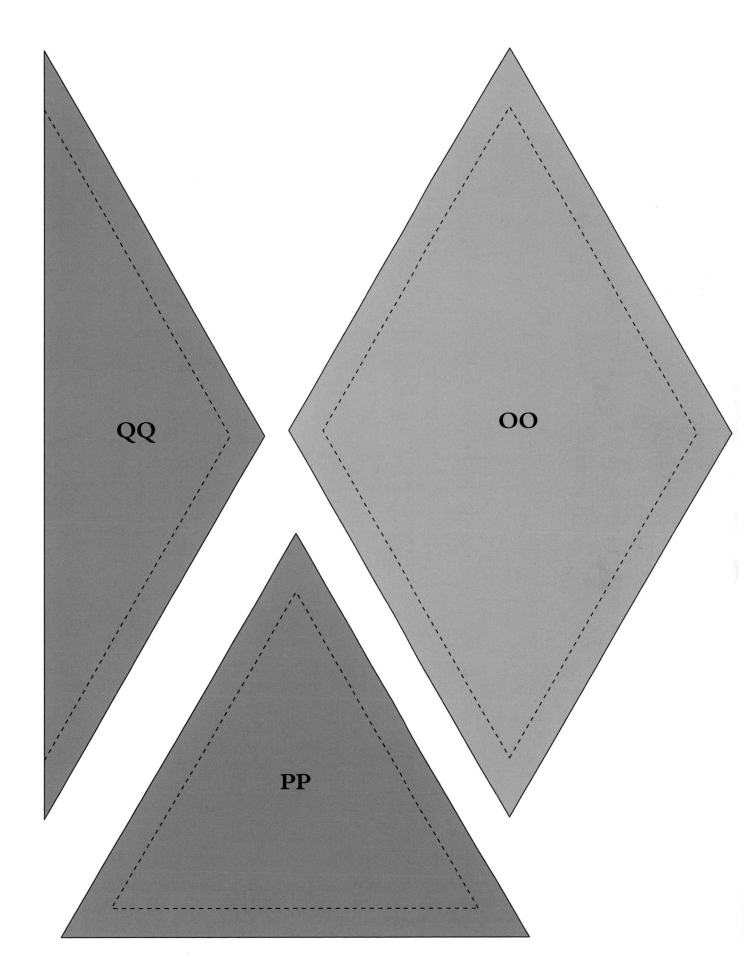

QQ

OO

PP

Welcome Home Stars Quilt

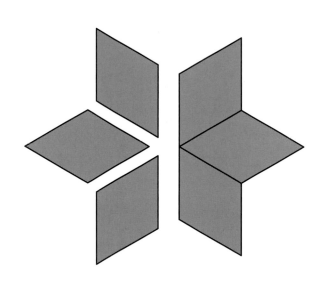

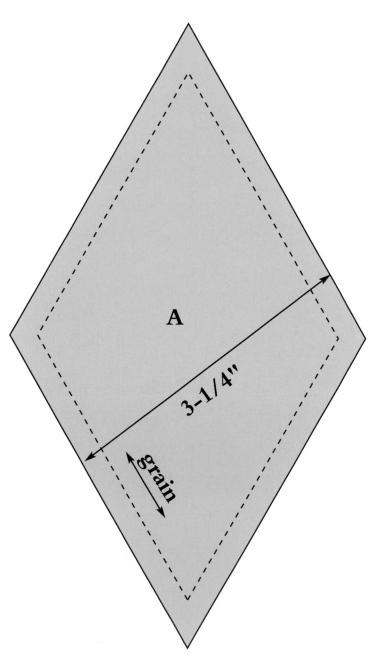

A

3-1/4"

grain

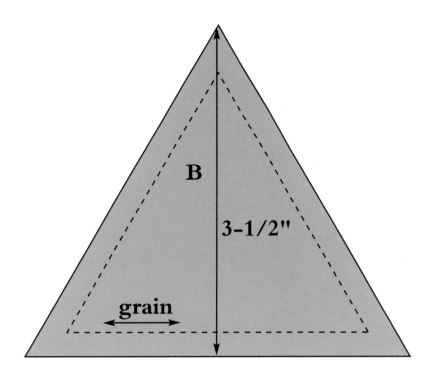

B

3-1/2"

grain

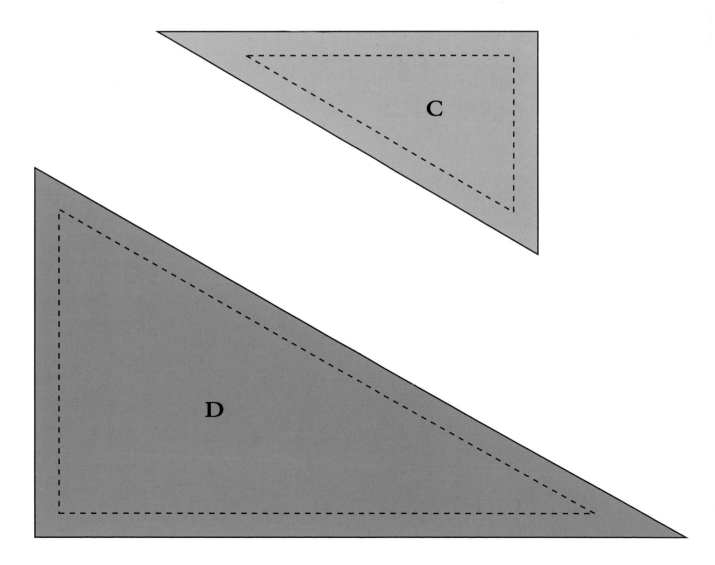

C

D

Katzahyden Quilt

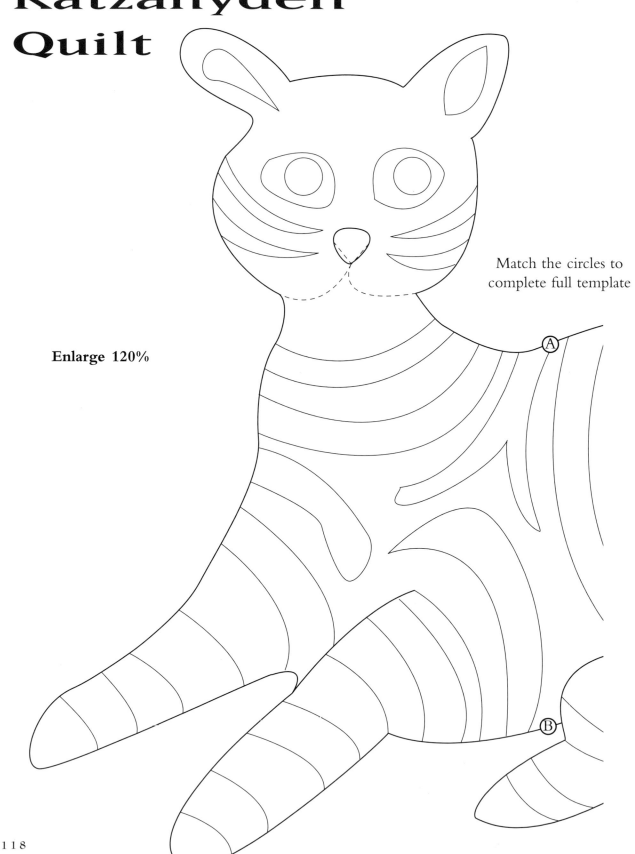

Enlarge 120%

Match the circles to
complete full template

Ⓐ

Ⓑ

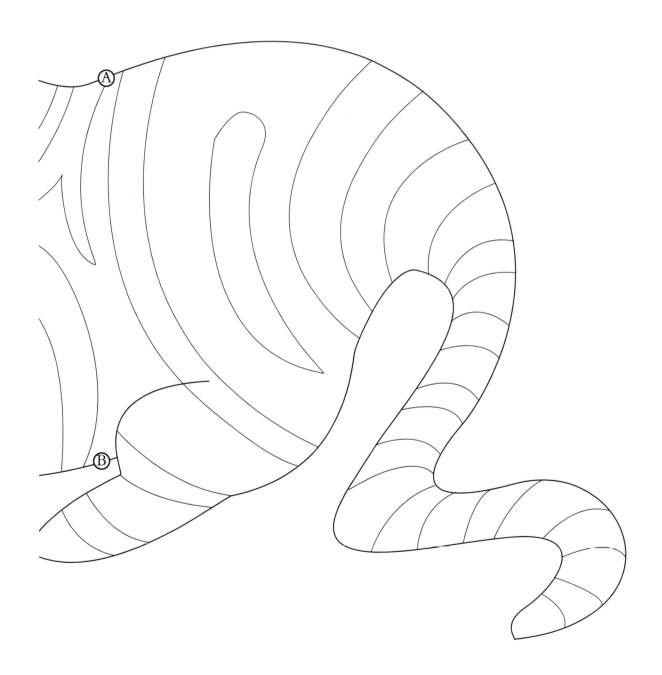

Schoolhouse Quilt

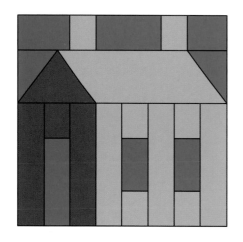

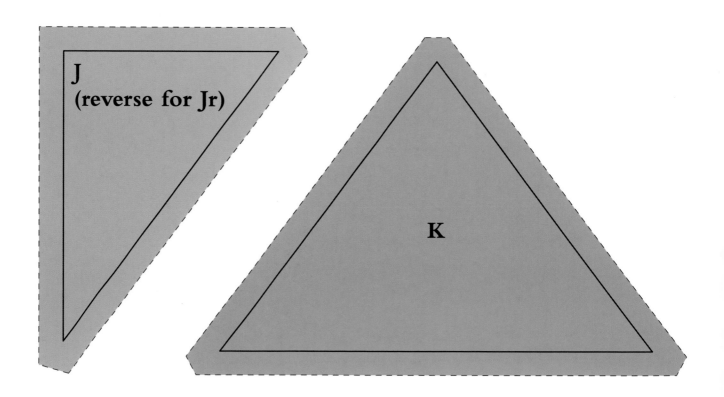

J
(reverse for Jr)

K

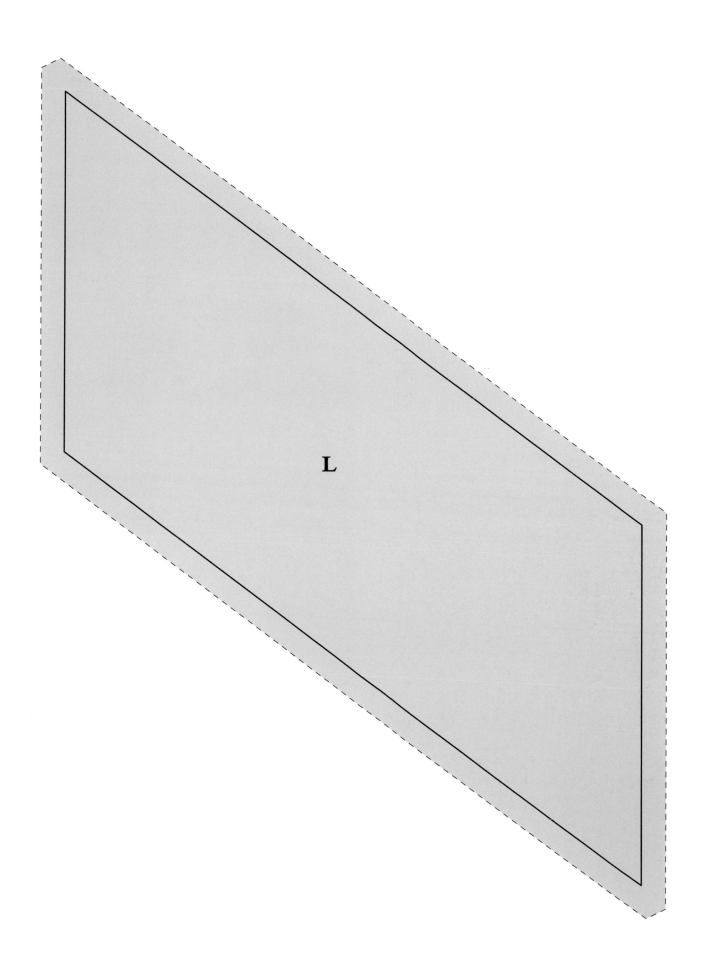

L

Acknowledgments

I would like to acknowledge with gratitude the people and organizations who helped me with my contribution to this book:

Lotus Stack, Liza Prior Lucy, Corienne Kramer, Sally Davis, Rebekah Lynch, Lynn Witzenburg, Pauline Smith, Yvonne Edwards, Belinda Mably, Brandon Mably, Marlene Heuertz, Marjon Schaefer, Landauer Corporation, Margaret Sindelar, Barbara Dickerson, Roxanne LeMoine, Westminster Fibers, Ehrman, Rowan, and Designers Guild.

A special thank you to Debbie Patterson for her photography.

Kaffe Fassett

The fabrics used in the pillows are Kaffe Fassett's Indian Stripe, Chard, Gazania, Roman Glass, Beads, and Pebbles fabrics.

Where to Buy

PATCHWORK FABRICS AND KITS:

WESTMINSTER FIBERS,
5 Northern Boulevard,
Amherst, NH 03031,
U.S.A.
Tel: (603) 886-5041,
Fax: (603) 886-1056.
ROWAN, Green Lane Mill,
Holmfirth, Huddersfield,
West Yorkshire HD7 1RW,
U.K.
Tel: (44) (1484) 681 881,
Fax: (44) (1484) 687 920.

NEEDLEPOINT KITS:

U.S.A.: *EHRMAN TAPESTRY,* 5300 Dorsey Hall Drive,
Suite 110, Ellicott City, MD 21042. Tel: toll-free order line
(888) 826-8600, customer service (410) 884-7944.
Fax: (410) 884-0598. E-mail: usehrman@mail.clark.net
U.K.: *EHRMAN (SHOP),* t14-16 Lancer Square, Kensington
Church Street, London W8 4EH, England.
Shop tel: (44) (171) 937 8123, Telephone ordering:
(44) (181) 573 4891, Fax: (44) (171) 937 8552.
Canada: *POINTERS,* 99 Yorkville Ave., Unit 103, Toronto,
Ontario M5R 3K5. Tel: (416) 962-9998 or (800) 465-5290,
Fax: (416) 962-6889.
Australia: *TAPESTRY ROSE,* PO Box 366, Canterbury Victoria
3126. Tel: (011) (61) 3 9804 0606.
New Zealand: *QUALITY HANDCRAFTS,* PO Box 1486,
Auckland. Tel: (64) (9) 411 8645, Fax: (64) (9) 307 1766.
South Africa: *SPEAKERS INTERNATIONAL,* Box 92043,
Norwood 2117. Tel: (27) 11 640 6722.

DECORATOR FABRICS:

DESIGNERS GUILD,
Osborne & Little, Inc.,
979 Third Ave., Ste. 520,
New York, NY 10022, U.S.A.
Tel: (212) 751-3333.

YARNS:

WESTMINSTER FIBERS,
5 Northern Boulevard,
Amherst, NH 03031, U.S.A.
Tel: (603) 886-5041.
Fax: (603) 886-1056
ROWAN, Green Lane Mill,
Washpit, Holmfirth,
Huddersfield HD7 1RW,
West Yorkshire, U.K.
Tel: (01484) 681 881.
Fax: (01484) 687 920.

PHOTO CREDITS:

CRAIG ANDERSON PHOTOGRAPHY: All photos in
Chapter 5. Flat shots on pages 87, 91, 95, 99, and 102-103.
DEBBIE PATTERSON: All other photography.
The inset shots on pages 10–13, courtesy of Random House
UK, were previously published in Kaffe Fassett's *Glorious
Patchwork* and *Glorious Interiors.*

For more information visit: www.kaffefassett.com

Photographed at the Minneapolis Institute of Arts

Photographed at the Minneapolis Institute of Arts

Photographed at the Minneapolis Institute of Arts

Photographed at the Minneapolis Institute of Arts